amy willcock's
aga know-how

amy willcock's aga know-how

lifting the lid on your aga

EBURY
PRESS

First published in Great Britain in 2003

3 5 7 9 10 8 6 4

Text © Amy Willcock 2003

Amy Willcock has identified her right to be identified as the author of this work
under the Copyright, Designs and Patents Act 1988.

First published by Ebury Press
Random House, 20 Vauxhall Bridge Road, London SW1V 2SA

Random House Australia (Pty) Limited
20 Alfred Street, Milsons Point, Sydney, New South Wales 2061, Australia

Random House New Zealand Limited
18 Poland Road, Glenfield, Auckland 10, New Zealand

Random House South Africa (Pty) Limited
Endulini, 5A Jubilee Road, Parktown 2193, South Africa

The Random House Group Limited Reg. No. 954009

www.randomhouse.co.uk

A CIP catalogue record for this book is available from the British Library.

Editor: Gillian Haslam
Illustrations: Hannah Popham

ISBN 0 091 895 839

Papers used by Ebury Press are natural, recyclable products made from wood grown in sustainable forests.

Typeset by Palimpsest Book Production Limited,
Polmont, Stirlingshire
Printed and bound by Mackays of Chatham, Chatham, Kent

Amy Willcock is the new writer for the contemporary Aga cook. She is the bestselling author of *Aga Cooking* and *Amy Willcock's Aga Baking* and has recently launched a cookware range with Mermaid. Amy runs Aga workshops and courses throughout the UK and also writes for *Agalinks* (the Aga website), *Aga Magazine* and *The Shooting Gazette*. Amy, her husband and John Illsley own three hotels, one of which, 'The George' on the Isle of Wight, has a Michelin-starred restaurant. Amy lives on the Isle of Wight with her husband and two daughters.

contents

introduction

You have now entered the 'Aga Zone'.

This book is the response to the countless emails, letters and requests from Aga owners and users who are desperate for any and all information they can get on Aga cooking. They all wanted an easy, quick, flick-through reference handbook that could be kept beside the Aga, to solve tiresome problems and to give great tips and hints at a glance – so here it is! I have packed in all the vital information every Aga user needs to know so this is the book you can't afford to be without. I love my Aga: any old cooker will feed you, but an Aga will teach you how to eat.

Thank you to all the Aga owners who have passed onto me their 'Aga wisdom', hints and tips. Keep the letters and e-mails coming – I look forward to them all! Which brings me to an old joke about a certain Gallic rugby team meeting the Aga Khan. On being introduced to the Aga Khan, the captain of the team said, 'I've never met you before but I've got one of your cookers!'

[signature]

The four stages of Aga Living:
Lager
Aga
Saga
Gaga

demystifying the aga

ask amy

Q Do I need another cooker as well as my Aga?

A No, if you are cooking the Aga way and using the 80/20 rule
(80 per cent of your cooking should be done in the ovens and only
20 per cent on the hot plates) you will be fine (but a separate hob
is useful).

Q Which size Aga should I buy?

A If you have the space, always go for a four-oven Aga. However,
two-oven Aga cookers are the most popular but we now also have
the option of a three-oven Aga which is the same size as the two-
oven, so the choice really is yours.

Q Do I need to turn off my Aga in summer?

A No. In today's well-ventilated houses it's usually not a problem – just open a window! With British weather as it is, I don't believe there is ever a need to turn it off. I have had some pretty damp, cold days even in the summer. Or if you live in hotter climes and don't have air conditioning, you may wish to turn it off in summer.

Q Can I stir-fry on an Aga?

A If you are a stir-fry freak, invest in a separate wok burner which allows flames to climb the sides – even a conventional cooker will not give you sufficiently intense heat. For the rest of us, the Boiling plate will suffice. Traditional woks may work adequately, but for best results use my universal pan (see page 63) which has a broad base, utilizing and collecting the heat quickly and efficiently. Pre-heat it in the Roasting Oven.

Q How do I clean the Aga?

A One of the best things about an Aga is that it cleans itself! But for detailed information on cleaning the lids and hotplates see page 50.

Q How do I grill on an Aga?

A There are two ways you can grill on an Aga. The first is to use the roasting tin and grill rack and hang the tin on the first set of runners so the foods being grilled are as near to the top as possible. The other method (which I use) is to heat up a ridged grill pan in the Roasting Oven so it is smoking, transfer it to the Boiling Plate, put your chops or fish or whatever it is you would like to grill in it and return the pan to the Roasting Oven floor and cook. Resist the temptation to move food around the pan once it is in for at least 2–3 minutes, then flip it over and continue to cook until the food is done.

Q My Aga always suffers from severe heat loss when I entertain or do Sunday lunch – what can I do?

A I cannot stress this enough – keep your lids down! Before you think about turning up the heat, examine your way of cooking and make sure you are following the 80/20 rule (see page 33). Check that the mercury is on the line in the thermometer and the correct level of heat is stored. If you really have examined your cooking methods and are confident you are using the Aga correctly, call in an Aga engineer.

Q What happens if I have a power cut?

A As the heat in an electric Aga is stored up like a storage heater, the cooking facility would be maintained for one day but as the fan would not operate, the oven heat would be considerably reduced, progressively getting worse with the duration of the power failure. Gas Aga cookers carry on indefinitely, but the power to the fan will turn off immediately. The oil-fired Aga cooker will remain alight, but will operate on a reduced heat until power is reinstated.

Q What happens if I spill water into the hot plate?

A Nothing, but do be more careful! And don't do it regularly! Any spillage will be absorbed into the insulation material. The one thing that is likely to cause a problem is milk because of the odour emitted when it dries out, so in the case of spilt milk it would be wise to remove the contaminated rockwool and replace it with fresh material.

Q How much does an Aga cost to run?

A These costs are only guidelines at the time of going to press and will depend on which company you buy your fuel from.
Natural gas: approximately £6–7 per week
Bottled gas: approximately £18 per week
Oil: approximately £12 per week
Electricity: approximately £4 per week

Q What is the Aga basic cooking and care kit?

A
2 grid shelves
1 plain shelf
1 full-size roasting tin
1 half-size roasting tin
Grills racks for each
Aga toaster
Steel wire brush
Pot of Astonish cleaning agent

If you are going to buy one extra piece of kit, I recommend my Oven Reach. You will find it indispensable.

aga envy

You never hear people enthuse about food cooked on other stoves like they do about Aga food – this is Aga envy.

everything tastes better cooked in the aga

The reason foods taste so much better when cooked in an Aga is because they retain valuable moisture, which is usually lost during conventional cooking. This is because, in some cases, the outer surface of the food is sealed by the Aga cooker's unique radiant heat. The air in a conventional oven is generally hotter than in an Aga; the hotter the air, the more moisture it will absorb, which can dry food out.

how it works

Every Aga is unique, whether it is brand new or old and battered. No two Aga cookers are the same because they are each hand-built, and some are old and some are new. Even old ones may have been reconditioned or had new parts or new insulations. So although all the principles, such as cooking methods and the way you use the Aga, are the same, the timings and 'movement' of the food around the Aga can vary enormously. You need to work out all the idiosyncrasies of your Aga.

It doesn't matter if they are powered by gas, electricity or oil as a burner heats them all in the same way. The heat from the burner unit is transferred to the ovens and hot plates where it is stored. When the insulated lids are down, they hold in the heat. When the lids are up, heat is lost.

All the ovens on the right-hand side of the Aga are externally vented, keeping cooking smells out of the kitchen and succulence in the food. The stored heat is released as radiant heat, which is what locks in the flavour and moisture, giving such superb results. Heat lost through cooking is automatically restored. The Aga is thermostatically controlled, so you don't need to worry about exact temperatures. I recommend new Aga users buy an oven thermometer and hang it in the middle of the ovens first thing in the morning to see what the temperatures are. Do this only once, just to give you an indication of the heat level.

> *'An Aga kitchen is a cleaner, cosier kitchen, a kitchen of which you will be very proud and in which you will work more happily, with far less toll on hands and nerves and body.'*
>
> Aga booklet, published in the 1950s

the heat is on

The heat indicator should be checked first thing in the morning, just to confirm that the Aga is up to heat. The mercury should sit on the black line (see diagram overleaf), which means that the Aga has its full amount of stored heat. Although I do know of Aga cookers where the mercury is in the black and they are fully up to heat, this is a rare occurrence. If this happens to a newly installed Aga, ask your Aga dealer to check it out. This is where the quirks of the Aga can be so different. It is quite usual for the

mercury to drop during cooking but don't worry as the heat will
automatically be restored.

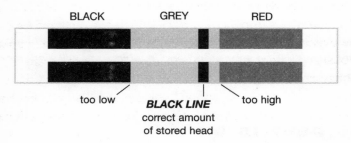

BLACK   GREY   RED

too low   **_BLACK LINE_**   too high
correct amount
of stored head

don't touch that dial

I only turn off my Aga for servicing, and once the temperature has
been reset and I am happy with the mercury position I don't touch
it until the next service (in my case, once a year). After installation
or servicing, make a note of the mercury position for the first few
mornings, and move the control up or down until the mercury
consistently reaches the black central line.

club 80 to 20

There is one golden rule in Aga cooking – *keep the lids down and cook in the ovens*. Around 80 per cent of cooking should be done in the ovens and only 20 per cent on the plates. The Aga cooker's combustion system, heat path and insulation schemes are designed on this premise. Once you have taken this on board, you will never suffer heat loss again. If you are doing a lot of cooking and need more heat, before you move the control knob, examine your cooking method.

remember to keep the lids down and cook in the ovens

What cooks where...

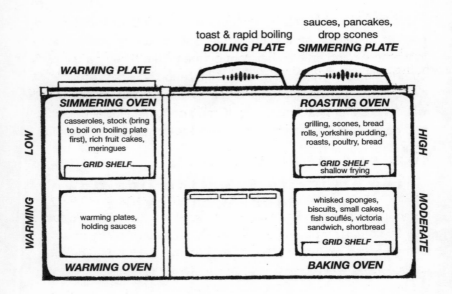

toast & rapid boiling
BOILING PLATE

sauces, pancakes,
drop scones
SIMMERING PLATE

WARMING PLATE

LOW

SIMMERING OVEN

casseroles, stock (bring to boil on boiling plate first), rich fruit cakes, meringues

GRID SHELF

ROASTING OVEN

grilling, scones, bread rolls, yorkshire pudding, roasts, poultry, bread

GRID SHELF
shallow frying

HIGH

WARMING

warming plates, holding sauces

whisked sponges, biscuits, small cakes, fish souflés, victoria sandwich, shortbread

GRID SHELF

MODERATE

WARMING OVEN

BAKING OVEN

And now for the geeky bits...

the boiling plate

The Boiling Plate is situated directly over the burner, making it the hottest plate. It is used when you want a fierce or high heat to bring foods to the boil or for stir-frying. Bread is toasted on it using the Aga Toaster. It is also where a Range Kettle is brought up to the boil.

the simmering plate

The Simmering Plate gives off a gentle heat ideal for simmering, but you can also use it like a griddle. Season it just as you would a new frying pan by putting a little vegetable oil on a piece of kitchen paper and wiping the plate's surface. Do this two or three times, leaving the lid up so that some of the oil burns off and does not leave an oily build-up. If you don't use the plate as a griddle for a while, re-season before use.

the biggest advantage of the simmering plate is that you can cook directly on it

To cook on the plate, lift the lid a few minutes before cooking to reduce the heat a little, wipe the surface with a small amount of oil and proceed with cooking. Remember, too much oil makes smoke! I cook pancakes, fried eggs, toasted sandwiches and tortillas like this. I always use the round pre-cut piece of Bake-O-Glide (see page 67) on the Simmering Plate. This eliminates the need for seasoning the plate and needs little, if any, oil, giving a low-fat cooking option.

Always close the lids promptly on both plates when you have finished using them, otherwise precious heat escapes. Each plate takes three large saucepans.

'Farmers use the simmering plate lids for hatching out pheasants' eggs, for pampering pedigree piglets with pneumonia, for saving three-day-old chicks from freezing, and other humane purposes, which their ingenuity suggests, and the good nature of their wives permits.'

Aga booklet, published in the 1950s

the warming plate

Available only on the 4-oven Aga, the Warming Plate is to the left of the Boiling Plate and is a very useful area for warming awkwardly shaped serving dishes and teapots. It is also great for resting large joints of roasted meat.

the aga ovens

The 2-oven Aga has a Roasting Oven and a Simmering Oven. The 4-oven Aga has a Roasting Oven, a Baking Oven, a Simmering Oven and a Warming Oven. The 3-oven Aga has recently been launched. It is basically the same as a 2-oven Aga with the addition of a Baking Oven. At the time of going to press, it is only available for use with LPG and natural gas, with a conventional flue.

the runners in the ovens are always counted from the top downwards

As there are no dials to control the temperatures, *food is cooked by position and timing*. If you think in those terms, adapting conventional recipes will become second nature. Looking at food while it is cooking is not a problem because the cast iron ovens retain the heat all around the inside of the oven and opening the door will not result in sudden heat loss.

the roasting oven

The Roasting Oven is the hottest oven with four different areas of cooking space:

High: top of the oven
Middle: centre of the oven
Low: near the bottom
Floor: the oven floor

What cooks where?

The oven is slightly hotter on the left side, which is near the burner.

High: the top of the oven is perfect for cooking foods that require a very high heat, such as grilled bacon and Yorkshire puddings, or for crisping up the tops of cottage pies or browning meats.

Middle: this is where joints of meat are cooked. Timings for roasts cooked here are the same as for conventional cookers. However, some roasts can be started here and then finished off in the Simmering Oven, but timings will be longer. For 2-oven Aga owners, this is the area to use for baking but you will need an item of cookware called an Aga Cake Baker (see page 117). It is essential for cakes that need more than 40 minutes' baking time. The cake baker is an 'oven within an oven', creating a moderate temperature for a longer amount of time. For cakes requiring less than 40 minutes, using the Cold Plain Shelf in the Roasting Oven creates a moderate oven temperature, but only for about 20–30 minutes. Once the plain shelf absorbs the oven's heat, it is useless until it is taken out and cooled. The Plain Shelf must not be stored in the Aga. It must go into the Aga cold. Four-oven Agas do not require a cake baker as they have a Baking Oven. Crumbles, muffins and cookies also cook well here.

Low: this is the part of the oven where roast potatoes, bread and sponge cakes are cooked. When making sponge cakes, do not use the cake baker; instead use heavy-based tins and place the grid shelf on the floor of the Roasting Oven and the plain shelf on the second set of runners just above, to cut the heat and create a moderate oven temperature.

Floor: think of the Roasting Oven floor as an extension of the hot plates – anything you can cook on the hot plates you can do on the Roasting Oven floor. Use it to fry foods such as onions or eggs or for browning meats. Heat a frying pan with a little oil in it on the floor of the Roasting Oven; add your ingredients and fry.

Do not put wooden or Bakelite-handled pans into the Roasting Oven. A good item of cookware to invest in is the Aga Grill Pan. By heating it up in the Roasting Oven you can 'grill' foods in it. I use this part of the oven the most. Bread can be baked directly on the floor with fantastic results, also pastry tarts and pies.

the baking oven

This oven is only available with the 3- or 4-oven Aga cookers. It is perfect for all baking as it is a moderate oven. It can also be used like the Roasting Oven but with longer cooking times. The top of the oven is slightly hotter.

What cooks where?

Top of the oven: small cakes are cooked to perfection.

Centre: for brownies, muffins, biscuits, breads and crumbles. It is also the right temperature for baking fish.

Bottom: when cooking soufflés or cheesecakes here, they must be off the floor. Slide a grid shelf onto the oven floor and stand the tin or dish on the grid shelf.

the simmering oven

This is the slow oven. On the 2-oven Aga it is on the bottom right; on the 4-oven Aga it is on the top left. On the 2-oven Aga it has three sets of runners; on the 4-oven model there is only one set in the middle. The gentle heat of the Simmering Oven is ideal for slow cooking and cooking overnight. Everything to be cooked in this oven, apart from meringues and a few other recipes, must be started either on the hot plates or in the Roasting Oven and brought up to the boil before going into the Simmering Oven. Saucepans must have tight-fitting flat lids that can be stacked one on top of the other. It is fine to put wooden and Bakelite-handled pans in the Simmering Oven.

What cooks where?

Centre: this is where casseroles, soups and stocks are made. Bring to the boil on the Boiling Plate, then transfer to the Simmering Oven. Roasts such as lamb and pork can be started in the Roasting Oven, and then transferred to the Simmering Oven, leaving valuable space in the Roasting Oven for other dishes. Rice puddings and baked custards are also started in the Roasting Oven, and then transferred to the Simmering Oven for slow, gentle cooking. The temperature is also just right for steamed puddings.

Bottom: if you don't have a Baking Oven, this is where fruitcakes and meringues are cooked. Pinhead oatmeal can be brought to the boil on the Boiling Plate, then placed on a grid shelf on the floor of the oven and left overnight for creamy porridge the next morning. This is the best place for drying fruits and vegetables, such as tomatoes and mushrooms, or infusing oils.

Floor: the floor of the Simmering Oven is perfect for cooking rice and root vegetables. The Aga way of cooking for rice (see page 142) results in delicious fluffy rice, while the Aga method for root vegetables (see page 93) is extremely easy and nutritious.

The Aga is perfect for people with a hectic lifestyle as it waits for you and there is no worry about ruining or burning foods. If you are delayed, the food can wait patiently in the Simmering Oven and still taste great.

the warming oven

Available in the 4-oven Aga only, this is primarily a place to keep things warm. As well as reviving the occasional orphaned lamb, it is where plates are warmed, and wet shoes stuffed with newspapers are dried out. It can, of course, dry out fruits and vegetables like the Simmering Oven but they will take much longer.

I have recently had a cold water tap fitted above my Aga. If you are having an Aga installed in your kitchen, it's well worth considering this as it makes filling kettles and pots and pans so easy.

New Aga-oven users sometimes find they burn their arms when using the ovens. The easy way to avoid this is to use the Oven Reach (see page 63) to retrieve pans from the back of the ovens and always to wear gauntlets.

who left the
lids up?

There is one question that crops up at every workshop or demonstration I do: 'Halfway through cooking Sunday lunch I find I run out of heat when cooking the roast potatoes or Yorkshire pudding. The mercury zooms down the thermometer. How can I prevent heat loss?'

The answer is simply to examine your method of cooking. Usually when people ask me this, I throw the question back at them and ask how many rounds of toast they've cooked, how many kettles have they boiled, and whether they've cooked a full breakfast using the plates rather than the ovens.

Heat loss often occurs if you use the hot plates too much beforehand. Perhaps you cooked breakfast on top rather than in the ovens that morning? Or par-boiled potatoes on the Boiling Plate instead of in the Simmering Oven. Check how much the lids are up. Remember to stick to the golden rule of 80 per cent of cooking to be done in the ovens and 20 per cent on the plates.

If you still experience problems after checking you are doing everything correctly, you are probably not planning your cooking timetable for the menu you have chosen. For instance, Yorkshire pudding can be cooked first thing in the morning when the ovens are at their hottest and successfully re-heated just before serving. Roast potatoes can be cooked up to their final 20 minutes the day before and then blasted in the Roasting Oven. And even green vegetables can be blanched the day before, ready to be re-heated the next day just before serving. Good cooking, whether it is on an Aga or conventional cooker, is all about planning and preparation.

planning and preparation

Make full use of the ovens by planning your oven space.

An easy way of doing this is to use the plain shelf. Put the shelf on your work surface and arrange the pieces of cookware you need to use on top of it or put the empty cookware you plan to use inside the oven. Take into account grid shelves and, if you can, stack pots and pans. My Rangeware pots and pans are made with flat lids for this reason, but if you are using conventional saucepans, invert the lids if possible and carry on stacking (but check that the lids will be safe and not fall in). When stacking pans, always point the handles in the same direction and use tins that fit directly onto the runners for maximum oven capacity.

When you fill the warming or simmering ovens, try to put the foods you are serving first at the front.

Try to plan your menu around your Aga. Consider logistics. Invariably food moves around the Aga, usually ending in the Warming or Simmering Ovens, on the Warming Plate or on protected hot plate lids. Plan to use the space they leave in the ovens well. You may find that you cook food in a different order than usual as the safety net of the Simmering or Warming Ovens allows for greater flexibility. Decide which recipes can be cooked ahead and take into account thawing times and re-heating times if applicable. Serve some foods that can be completely prepared and cooked ahead and just need re-heating.

'Even feminine, domesticated Pamela, known as "Woman",
was enough of a Mitford to have John Betjeman at her feet
and her Aga painted blue to match her eyes.'
    The Mitford Girls by Mary S Lovell (Little Brown, 2001)

my biggest tip

Look at your dishes cooking and baking in the Aga frequently and don't be afraid to move the food around to another location in or on your Aga. If a hot plate is too hot, then move it. The recipe timings in my books are a guide and remember that every Aga is different. The Aga creates intuitive cooks because of this. You will learn to cook by instinct.

at-a-glance cooking methods

Boiling: Boiling Plate. Once boil is established, move to the Roasting Oven floor.

Simmering: start on the Boiling Plate, cover with a lid, then move to the Simmering Oven. To reduce liquids, remove lid and continue in the Simmering Oven.

Braising: bring up to the boil on the Boiling Plate for 5–10 minutes, and then move to the Simmering or Baking Oven.

Browning Meat: use the first set of runners in the Roasting Oven, and then move to the Roasting Oven floor.

Frying: use the Roasting Oven floor and first set of runners in the Roasting Oven.

Grilling: use the Aga grill pan on the Roasting Oven floor or on the Boiling Plate.

Poaching: bring to the boil on the Boiling Plate, then move to the Roasting or Simmering Oven depending on food being poached (poach eggs on the Simmering Plate).

Roasting: Roasting, Baking and Simmering Ovens – use Roasting Oven for conventional timings; Baking and/or Simmering Ovens for slow roasting.

Steaming: start on the Boiling Plate or in the Roasting Oven, cover, and then move to the Simmering Oven.

stir-frying on your aga

The Boiling Plate provides the intense heat needed for stir-frying. Traditional woks may work adequately, but for best results use my universal pan which has a broad base, collecting the heat quickly and efficiently (see page 164 for stockists). Pre-heat the pan in the Roasting Oven.

foods at-a-glance

Below are some helpful general cooking positions.

Jacket potatoes: third set of runners or Roasting Oven floor.

Roasted vegetables: first set of runners or Roasting Oven floor.

Rice: bring up to the boil on the Boiling Plate, cover, and then transfer to the Simmering Oven. In general, most quantities of rice (unless very large) take about 20 minutes.

Pasta: boil on the Boiling Plate.

Cookies and biscuits: fourth set of runners with the Cold Plain Shelf on the second set of runners in the Roasting Oven. Third set of runners in the Baking Oven.

Muffins: grid shelf on floor of Roasting Oven with Cold Plain Shelf above, or on fourth set of runners with Cold Plain Shelf on second set of runners. In Baking Oven on third set of runners.

Bread: directly on the Roasting Oven floor.

Toasted sandwiches: use the round Bake-O-Glide and cook directly on the Simmering Plate.

20 minutes seems to be the magic cooking time for many dishes

hints and tips

- If a dish needs more than 7 minutes of cooking use one of the Aga ovens, not the hotplates.
- Buy two really reliable and accurate timers, preferably digital. Timers are crucial to the Aga cook. Or buy a timer on a long cord so that you can wear it around your neck – this means you will hear the timer wherever you are.
- Tie a red ribbon around the rail or above so that it catches your eye and reminds you something is in the oven. A magnet with a note attached works well too.
- Always pre-heat the Aga toaster to prevent bread sticking to it.
- To save time and energy, pre-heat pans in the Roasting Oven (do not put in saucepans with wooden or plastic handles).

- Protect open lids from splatters with a tea towel draped over the back (remove before closing the lid).
- For 2-oven Aga owners, plan to do your baking when the ovens will be cooler, such as after a heavy cooking session.
- The cooking times for older Aga cookers may have to be adjusted, because insulation originally used was not as efficient as it is now. Newer Aga models benefit from modern technology.
- In some kitchens with older Aga cookers you will see a stack of old pennies next to or even on top of the Aga – they are very useful for slightly lifting saucepans and creating the right temperature for certain dishes.

converting recipes for aga use

Converting conventional recipes for Aga use is easy. Just remember how the heat is distributed in each oven and once you decide where the food is to be cooked, adjust the timings accordingly. I tend to underestimate the time by roughly

10 minutes, as I can put the dish back in for a little longer if necessary.

all aga cooking is done by timing and position

Take a standard muffin recipe. The ingredients and method are exactly the same. The recipe calls for an oven pre-heated to 180°C/350°F/gas 4 and a cooking time of 40–45 minutes.

For the 2-oven Aga:
There is no need to pre-heat the oven as the Aga is always ready to cook. Make the batter according to the recipe, and pour the mix into the muffin tin. I would use the lower/bottom half of the Roasting Oven, but not the Roasting Oven floor. Place the grid shelf on the floor of the Roasting Oven and the cold plain shelf (to make a moderate oven temperature of 180°C/350°F/gas 4) on the second set of runners. Estimate the time at 30 minutes, but it may take up to 45 minutes if the oven is not right up to temperature.

Check after about 25 minutes. They are done when pale golden and shrinking away from the sides of the tin.

For the 3- and 4-oven Aga:
As above but cook in the Baking Oven omitting the cold plain shelf until it is needed (probably 20–25 minutes into the cooking time).

aga temperatures

These are the typical centre-oven temperatures:

Roasting Oven
Hot – approximately 240–260°C/475–500°F/gas 8–9

Baking Oven
Moderate – approximately 180–200°C/350–400°F/gas 4–6

Simmering Oven
Slow – approximately 135–150°C/200–300°F/gas 1

Warming Oven
Warm – approximately 70–100°C/150–200°F/gas 1/4

aga love

an aga is for life, not just for christmas!

This is where I have to come clean and confess my Aga only gets cleaned properly when I do my demonstrations! Treat most of the advice below as optional.

To have a clean Aga is simple: avoid getting it dirty in the first place! If you use the ovens for cooking foods that splatter (such as during frying and grilling), the hot plates will stay clean. Pushing pans to the rear of the ovens will keep the aluminium door clean as well. Keep a damp cloth ready to wipe up spills as they happen. Acidic liquids and milk can cause pitting to the enamel top. Don't drag pans across the top or the surface will eventually scratch.

cleaning the ovens

it gives me great pleasure to report that oven cleaning doesn't really exist with an aga!

The ovens self-clean because the constant high heat means that food spills carbonise and only need to be brushed out with the wire brush. The Aga doors must NEVER be immersed in water as this would destroy the insulation.

If you have a metal nozzle on your vacuum cleaner, you can use it to suck out the carbonised bits that gather at the bottom of the oven.

To clean the doors, simply lay out a double thickness of tea towels on a flat surface and then carefully lift off the doors from the hinges. Use gauntlets to move the doors, as they will be very hot. Lay the doors on the tea towels enamel side down and leave to cool for a few minutes. Using a damp wire wool scouring pad and a little washing-up liquid, firmly go over the inside of the door – it will scratch the aluminium but it won't harm it. Wipe it clean and replace the doors on the hinges.

To clean the outside of the oven doors and the enamelled front and top, use a mild cream cleaner. Lightly apply it with a damp cloth, then wipe with a dry cloth to polish off any residue. A silicone polish can also be used on the front and top of the cooker to help control the dust. This is a good idea for darker-coloured cookers, where the dust tends to be more visible.

cleaning the hot plates

Clean the hot plate surfaces with the wire brush. Food will burn off and all that is needed is to clear away any carbonised bits that will interfere with the contact between saucepan bottoms and the hot surface. It's useful to keep the wire brush handy when making toast so that you can clear away breadcrumbs immediately.

To clean the inside of the Simmering Plate lid, lift the lid and leave open for a few minutes to cool slightly, then place a grid shelf over the hot plate and the plain shelf on top of the grid shelf. This will reduce the heat, allowing easier cleaning in the middle of the lid, and is also a safety precaution in case your hand slips. Use a soapy wire wool pad and a damp cloth. The inside of the lid will scratch but it will not affect the cooker's performance. The Boiling Plate lid rarely needs cleaning as the intense heat keeps it clean.

Clean the chromium lids with a soapy damp cloth and buff with a clean dry tea towel. Do not use wire wool or any harsh abrasives on the chrome. To avoid the tops of the lids being scratched, either use the specially designed round Aga oven pads or a folded tea towel to protect them if you place dishes on top. Don't put heavy pans or tins on them as this may dent them.

If you find grease collects around the very edge of the plates, you can use a craft knife to remove by scraping gently, but take care not to scratch the enamel.

servicing your aga

Always use an authorised Aga distributor to service your Aga. If you move into a house with an Aga already in situ, try to find out its service history from the previous owners, plus the telephone number of the company that services it. Gas and electric Aga cookers should be serviced once a year and oil-fuelled Aga cookers every six months. The standard check and service will take about an hour.

The night before a service, remember to turn off your Aga so that it cools down. Turn the burner off and leave the pilot on (refer to the inside of the burner compartment door). After servicing, the Aga engineer will re-light the Aga for you.

crème de la crème

Did you know that 60 per cent of all Aga cookers ever sold have been cream in colour? Until 1956 cream was the only colour available.

second-hand rose

There are lots of companies selling second-hand and re-conditioned Aga cookers. Most Aga distributors sell second-hand Aga cookers from clients who are upgrading their Aga cooker so it is worth enquiring about these. However there are a few key questions you should ask:

- How old is the Aga, how many owners has it had and does it contain asbestos products?
- Does it come with a guarantee?

- Is it going to be fully installed by an Aga-trained engineer? Are they CORGI registered (a legal requirement)? Aga cookers are designed to be built on site so do not accept one that has been moved fully assembled.
- Will the company service the Aga?
- Has the cooker ever been converted from one fuel to another?
- Have any parts been replaced? If so, have they been replaced with genuine Aga parts? If not, have the parts just been cleaned up and painted?
- Has it been re-finished? Is it painted or vitreous enamelled?
- Is there a charge for a colour change?
- Is cookware supplied with the Aga?
- What installation charges are included in the price? Assembly charges? Delivery charges? Do they deliver directly to the kitchen?
- Will the Aga have the Aga-Rayburn stamp of approval?

buying a used aga can mean buying a nightmare so do beware

converted aga cookers

Do beware of converted Aga cookers. A converted Aga is usually one that has been converted from solid fuel to oil or occasionally to gas. As every Aga is hand-built to specific fuel requirements, it is always a risk to own a converted Aga for two reasons – safety and performance.

The safety of the cooker could be affected by the altering or modifying of the product and will nullify the approval and, in the case of gas-fired products, could be illegal. The performance of the Aga could certainly be affected as the original performance is difficult to achieve if modifications have been made.

Age is a consideration. Some Aga cookers are 40 years old and work perfectly well in their original environment. However, when moved or converted to suit a new home they may not work as they should and the cost can be almost as much as a new one.

In 1994 the BBC Watchdog programme reported on buying converted Aga and Rayburn cookers. The programme alerted potential Aga purchasers of the problems and risks of buying second-hand. The report discovered that in some cases the second-hand Aga cost as much as a new one by the time the necessary conversions were made to make it safe.

For more information, do contact Aga-Rayburn (see page 164) because they produce an extremely comprehensive booklet on buying an Aga cooker.

If you have guests staying, try to make them 'aga aware' so scratches, spills and dents are avoided.

pots and pans

Each new Aga comes with the basic Aga kit:

2 grid shelves
Large roasting tin and grill rack
Half-size roasting tin and grill rack
1 plain shelf
1 toaster
1 wire brush

I recommend you invest in a few more half-size roasting tins, and 2-oven Aga owners would find another plain shelf useful if they plan to do a lot of baking.

rangeware

My range of cookware came about because there were certain items I wanted but couldn't find. We have produced a range of cookware for all range cooking. All the pots and pans can be used

on conventional cookers as well as on and in the Aga. It is called
Rangeware, is made by Mermaid and is manufactured in the UK.
For stockists see page 164.

amy willcock's rangeware

1 x 9 litre stainless steel stockpot *
2 x 16 cm hard anodised saucepan with stainless steel stacking lid *
2 x 18 cm hard anodised saucepan with stainless steel stacking lid *
2 x 20.5 cm hard anodised saucepan with stainless steel stacking lid *
3 x 1 litre shallow casserole with stainless steel stacking lid *
1 x non-stick milk pan *
1 x cake baker * (2-oven Aga owners only)
2 x half-size hard anodised shallow baking tray (fits directly onto
the runners) *
2 x full-size hard anodised baking tray (fits directly onto the
runners and can be used as a plain shelf)
2 x half-size hard anodised tray bake (fits onto runners)
1 x full-size hard anodised tray bake (fits onto runners)
1 x cast iron grill pan *

1 x 1.5 litre aluminium kettle, interior non-stick coated *
1 x 3.5 litre aluminium kettle, interior non-stick coated
1 x cast iron sauté pan
2 x 18 cm loose-bottomed hard anodised sponge tins *
2 x 20 cm loose-bottomed hard anodised sponge tins *
1 x hard anodised universal pan and lid *
1 x hard anodised deep roasting tin
1 x oven reach (very useful for getting tarts, breads and pizzas out
of the oven) *

Don't be alarmed at the size of this list – you can collect pans over
the years and don't need to buy them all at once. I have marked
the items I consider essential with an asterisk.

saucepans and casseroles

One of the first things all new Aga owners want to know is whether
they have to buy new saucepans. The easy answer is no, because
most people will have some suitable cookware already. However,

to maximise the Aga, use my Rangeware collection. They have machined-flat, heavy ground bases and reach boiling point very quickly, thereby conserving heat. Pans that are not suitable waste valuable heat time and energy and there will be a marked difference in cooking times. Cast iron, earthenware, ceramic and copper are all suitable for the Aga. Glass Pyrex can also be used in the ovens on the grid shelves.

To test if your existing saucepans are suitable for the Aga, fill each one with cold water and put it on the Boiling Plate. Hold each side of the pan down and see if the pan rocks. If the pan is flat, tiny bubbles appear uniformly over the bottom of the surface. It is not flat if the bubbles appear only in certain areas of the pan.

Saucepans with wooden or Bakelite handles are not suitable for the Roasting Oven. Buy pans that are fully ovenproof and that can be used anywhere on the Aga. Saucepans and casseroles should be as wide as possible so that they cover most of the hot plate surface. The flat lids on my pans enable stacking in the ovens, giving masses of room for cooking.

baking tins

When buying tins for the Aga, make sure that they slide onto the runners. This will mean the full capacity of the ovens will be used. The one tin that I use constantly is the half-size shallow hard anodised baking tray. The full-size one can also be used as a plain shelf. They are sufficiently heavy duty to use on the hot plates and ideal for things like roasting potatoes.

Make sure muffin and other specialised tins are also as heavy duty as possible. Cake tins must be heavy duty. As dark colours absorb heat more quickly than lighter, you may find in some cases a darker cake tin will require a slightly shorter cooking time than, say, a lighter aluminium cake tin.

kettles

To get the best from your kettle, buy a size that suits your needs. There is no point having the 3-litre kettle if your household only has two people in it. My 'baby' kettle is fantastic and is a must for everyday use. Bring out the hulking great kettle for large gatherings such as Christmas.

A common complaint about kettles is that they become pitted at the bottom and can take a long time to come to the boil. The first problem occurs when all the boiled water in the kettle is not used, and the water level is just topped up. This is bad practice as the boiled water leaves mineral deposits sitting on the base of the kettle which cause pitting. When this happens, it takes longer to bring water up to the boil and the kettle is less efficient. Using a smaller kettle means that you are more likely to use up all the water in it so you will fill it up with fresh water more often. If you are using a large kettle, only fill it with the amount of water needed for the job. If you live in a hard-water area, it is essential to descale the kettle once a week.

bake-o-glide

Bake-O-Glide changed my life! And it will change yours too! Use this amazing non-stick, re-useable paper to line tins, making cleaning a cinch, or on the Simmering Plate. It is dishwasher-safe and only small amounts of fat are needed, if at all, to make surfaces non-stick. Roast potatoes crisp up beautifully and the crunchy bits left in the tin lift off easily. It is available in rolls and in pre-cut sizes. I use the pre-cut circle on the Simmering Plate to fry eggs, cook pancakes and make toasted sandwiches. For your nearest stockist, call 01706 224790 and speak to Gary or his mum Marjorie.

turf and coop

vegetarians look away now!

Roasting a joint of meat in the Aga is always easy and the radiant heat locks in the flavour, making it a truly different eating experience altogether. For meats like lamb and pork, you can use the slow roasting method or cook it conventionally. For good cuts of meat, veal and beef, I suggest using the fast roasting method.

slow roasting method

Prepare the joint for cooking. Cut a couple of onions in half and put them into a tin lined with Bake-O-Glide. Sit the joint on top of the onions and slide the tin onto the fourth set of runners of the Roasting Oven for 30–40 minutes or until it begins to brown, then transfer to the Simmering Oven for approximately double the amount of conventional cooking time. Weigh the joint before cooking to calculate the timings.

conventional fast roasting method

Prepare the joint as for slow roasting and calculate the roasting time according to the cut and type of meat. When it is finished cooking, rest for 15–20 minutes before carving.

aga cooking times

Beef
Rare: 12 minutes per 450 g
Medium: 15 minutes per 450 g
Well done: 20 minutes per 450 g

Lamb
Pink in the middle: 15 minutes per 450 g
Well done: 20 minutes per 450 g

Pork
25 minutes per 450 g

Veal
15 minutes per 450 g

fillet of beef

This method of cooking a whole fillet of beef results in a beautifully rare middle.

For 900 g fillet, put about 2 tablespoons of dripping in the large roasting tin and place on the Roasting Oven floor. When the fat is smoking, transfer the tin to the Boiling Plate and seal the meat on all sides. The fat will splatter so keep a damp cloth handy to wipe up any mess. Remove the excess fat, then hang the tin on the third set of runners in the Roasting Oven. Cook for no more than 15–20 minutes. When the cooking time is up, take the fillet out of the oven and remove from the tin. Do not wash the tin. Wrap the meat very tightly in cling film, twisting the ends for a snug fit. Put the fillet onto a plate and leave it to rest for at least 20 minutes on top of the protected Simmering Plate. To serve the meat, remove the cling film, put the meat back into the tin and put the tin on the Roasting Oven floor for 8–10 minutes, just to heat it through. Serve straight away.

roast chicken

This method is suitable for roasting chicken and all poultry except large turkeys.

Line the roasting tin with Bake-O-Glide. Cut an onion in half (use two for a large chicken) and place the chicken on top of the onion. Stuff the cavity of the chicken with herbs, onion or lemon and season with salt and pepper. Rub over butter or oil or lay strips of bacon over the chicken; rub in more salt and pepper. Slide the tin onto the lowest set of runners in the Roasting Oven and set the timer. Check halfway through cooking and cover the chicken with foil if it is browning too quickly. To test if the chicken is cooked, pierce the thigh with a skewer; if the juices run clear, it is cooked. If they are pink or red, the chicken is not ready so cook for a little longer. Rest the chicken for 15 minutes before carving.

Approximate timings for roasting a whole chicken:

900 g chicken (small): 35–45 minutes
1.5 kg chicken (medium): 45–60 minutes
2 kg chicken (large): 1½–1¾ hours
3 kg chicken (very large): 2 hours

roast duck

Put the duck into a colander and pour over a kettle full of boiling water – this helps to start loosening the fat. Drain the duck and dry it really well with kitchen paper inside and out. Brush the duck with a little brandy (alcohol helps to dry out the skin, giving you a crispier finish).

Hang the duck up by its wings with a plate underneath in a place where (a) it won't be attacked by the cat and (b) there is a cool breeze (the air helps to keep the duck really dry). If you don't have anywhere like this, put it uncovered into the fridge. This can all be done a day in advance, but it must be left hanging for a minimum of 6 hours.

When you are ready to cook the duck, put it onto a grill rack in a roasting tin and hang it onto the third or fourth set of runners in the Roasting Oven and cook for 1–2 hours, depending how big the duck is. I like the meat practically falling away from the bones and really crispy skin, but if you want your duck rarer, only cook it for roughly an hour.

When the duck has finished cooking, remove it from the oven and allow it to rest for 5–10 minutes.

roast pheasant

Line the roasting tin with Bake-O-Glide. Place the bird(s) in the tin, rub generously with butter or lard (or even cover with the paper that the butter is wrapped in) and season with salt and pepper. If you wish, cover the breasts with bacon. Stuff the cavity of the pheasant with half an onion or apple and season with salt and pepper. Slide the tin onto the third set of runners of the Roasting Oven and set the timer for 45–50 minutes. Baste halfway through cooking. To test if the pheasant is cooked, pierce the thigh with a skewer; if the juices run clear, it is cooked. Be careful not to overcook game – as the fat content is lower, it does have a tendency to dry out.

roast partridge, grouse, woodcock, snipe and quail

Cook as for pheasant but adjust the cooking times and accompaniments.

Partridge: Roast for 30–35 minutes and serve with quince cheese or redcurrant jelly.

Grouse: Roast for 20–30 minutes and serve on croûtes of fried bread spread with the pan-fried liver of the grouse if you are lucky enough to have it.

Woodcock, snipe and quail: Roast for 12–15 minutes. Serve woodcock and snipe on croûtes (as for grouse). Quail is such a versatile bird that it can be served in almost any way you wish. As a guide, allow 1½ birds per person.

roast turkey

The Aga can accommodate a turkey weighing up to 12.5 kg and I
recommend using my deep roasting tin. There are two methods of
roasting turkey: the slow roasting method, which can be done
overnight, and the conventional method. The advantage of the
slow method is that you don't have to worry about the turkey and
the Roasting Oven will be available for cooking all the traditional
trimmings. Timings are approximate and very much depend of the
size of the bird. The timings may have to be increased for older
Aga cookers if you use the slow roasting method.

The conventional method of cooking the turkey will use up quite a
lot of heat so planning and preparation are very important.

preparing a fresh turkey
Wash the turkey with water and pat dry with kitchen towel. Stuff
only the neck end of the bird. Put a couple of onions into the
body cavity and season well with salt and pepper. Put the turkey

into the roasting tin. Do not truss the bird. Generously brush melted clarified butter all over the bird and season with salt. The secret of a succulent golden bird is in the basting. Leave the pot of clarified butter at the back of the Aga so that it is within easy reach for basting about every 30 minutes if cooking the bird conventionally.

slow roasting method

Place the roasting tin directly on the floor of the Roasting Oven and cook for about 1 hour or until the turkey is browned. A larger turkey may take longer to brown. It is essential to give the turkey a real blast of heat for a good amount of time for food safety. When it is browned, baste with the clarified butter and move to the Simmering Oven for the following times:

3.6–4.5 kg: 3–6 hours
5–7.25 kg: 5–8½ hours
7.25–9 kg: 8½–11 hours

9–11 kg: 11–13½ hours
11–12.8 kg: 13½–15½ hours
All times are approximate.

conventional or fast roasting method

Place the roasting tin on the floor of the Roasting Oven or hang on the last runner if it will fit. After about 1 hour, or when the turkey is browned, cover loosely with foil and cook for the following times:

3.6–4.5 kg: 1¾–2 hours

5–7.25 kg: 2–2½ hours

7.25–9 kg: 2½–3 hours

9–11 kg: 3½–4½ hours

11–12.8 kg 4½–5½ hours

All times are approximate

The turkey is done when the thigh juices run clear when pierced with a skewer. Rest the turkey for at least 20 minutes. A large bird will stay hot for a long time and can withstand a long resting time so take this into consideration when working out your cooking timetable.

When using the conventional roasting method, you can start cooking the turkey breast side down, turning it breast side up about 45 minutes before the end of the cooking time. This way of cooking the turkey ensures the breast meat will be even more succulent.

grilled chops

Heat the Aga grill pan on the floor of the Roasting Oven until it smokes. Season the chops with salt and pepper. Transfer the grill pan to the Boiling Plate. Add the chops and place the pan back on the Roasting Oven floor for 4–5 minutes, depending how thick the chops are. Turn the chops over and cook for a further 4–5 minutes until cooked through.

sausages

Lay the sausages on the grill rack in the roasting tin. Slide the tin onto the highest runners in the Roasting Oven and cook for 20–30 minutes, turning halfway through cooking so they are coloured on all sides.

spare ribs

Ribs taste better if they have been marinated for an hour before cooking. Drain the ribs from the marinade. Line a roasting tin with Bake-O-Glide and lay the ribs on top. Hang the tin from the fourth set of runners in the Roasting Oven and cook for 40 minutes. Pour your sauce over them and transfer to the Simmering Oven for 1–2 hours or until the meat is tender.

For crispy bacon, cook the rashers on Bake-O-Glide in a shallow baking tray on the Roasting Oven floor.

surf's up

The Aga is perfect for cooking fish as it locks in the juices at the same time as crisping up the skin. One of the amazing things about the Aga is that fish can easily be cooked in the same oven as, say, a fruit tart or sponge cake without the transference of smell or taste.

poaching fish

For a whole fish, such as a salmon, use the conventional fish kettle method. Make a court bouillon by filling a fish kettle with water, herbs, peppercorns and lemon halves, then put in the whole fish. Bring to the boil on the Boiling Plate (if the kettle is large, use the Simmering Plate as well). As soon as it has boiled for 5 minutes, remove the kettle from the heat and leave the fish to cool in the liquid. This method cooks fish really well and you can forget about it while it cools.

oven-steamed fish

Steaming fish in the Aga is easy. Lay a large piece of foil on a
shallow tin and butter the inside of the foil. Lay the fish on the
foil and season with herbs, lemons, salt and pepper. Spoon over
1 tablespoon of white wine or water, and then wrap up the foil
into a loose parcel, fully sealed but with enough room for steam
at the top. Slide the tin onto the third set of runners of the
Roasting Oven and cook for 10–12 minutes or until the fish is
cooked to your liking. Owners of 4-oven Agas can also use the
Baking Oven, although the fish will take slightly longer to
cook here.

frying fish in the roasting oven

Pour sunflower oil into a heavy-based shallow pan to a depth of
2–3 cm. Place the pan on the floor of the Roasting Oven and heat
until smoking. Batter the fish or coat in breadcrumbs. Remove the
pan from the oven, add the fish to the pan and return to the
Roasting Oven floor. Fry for a few minutes on each side in the pan
or until the batter or breadcrumbs are golden.

aga kippers

Place the kippers in a roasting tin. Add about a tablespoon of
water to the bottom of the tin and place a knob of butter on
top of each kipper. Cover with foil and cook in the Roasting
Oven for 8–10 minutes. If they are on the bone, they may
take longer.

shellfish

It is best to cook shellfish for as little time as possible. Things like mussels, clams, etc only need to be steamed open so cook on either the Boiling or Simmering Plate.

I roast lobster in the Roasting Oven, but you do have to be brave and not squeamish as you must drive a knife through their heads first. Of course you can boil them on the Boiling Plate as well.

Scallops are superb simply sealed in a smoking pan that has been heated in the Roasting Oven first, then moved to either the Boiling or Simmering Plate.

Always pre-heat your baking tray in the Roasting Oven before you put the fish on it so the fish starts to cook immediately.

eat your greens

Root vegetables can be cooked very successfully in the Aga, retaining most of their valuable vitamins as well as their taste. Once you learn the trick of cooking your veggies this way, you will never cook them any other way.

Cook green vegetables, such as French beans, peas, mange tout, etc, in the conventional way. Bring a pan of water to the boil and cook them in salted boiling water for as long you like, then drain and serve. However, when it comes to root vegetables, such as potatoes, carrots, etc, the Aga method is by far the best. Firstly, it eliminates lots of unwanted steam in the kitchen and, secondly, it conserves valuable heat.

underground vegetables

Prepare the vegetables, say potatoes, in the usual way. Peel or scrub them and put into a saucepan of salted water. Bring the saucepan to the boil on the Boiling Plate and cook with the lid on for 4–5 minutes. Remove the pan from the heat and drain off all the water. Replace the lid and put the pan on the Simmering Oven floor. The potatoes will take approximately 25–30 minutes to cook but the timing really does depend on the size of the vegetables being cooked. I usually cook carrots for about 15 minutes as I like them with a bit of a bite.

The amazing thing about this method of cooking vegetables is that if for some reason the meal is delayed, the vegetables happily sit in the Simmering Oven for up to 3 hours without burning. It is true to say they would be well done, but they would still be edible, neither falling apart nor burnt.

If you have ovenproof serving tureens with tight-fitting lids, you can use them like a saucepan. Once the veg have boiled for 4–5 minutes, drain, tip them into the tureen and cover. They will cook in the tureen in the Simmering Oven so all you have to do is season and carry them to the table.

get-ahead vegetables

This is a 'trick of the trade' tip – restaurants have been preparing vegetables like this for years.

Have ready a large bowl of water with some ice in it. Put it to one side. Cook your vegetables for 2–3 minutes in rapidly boiling water so they are tender. Using a slotted spoon, transfer them from the boiling water straight into the bowl of iced water (this is what is meant when a recipe says 'blanch'). The iced water stops the vegetables cooking further and helps them retain their colour. Then drain well on kitchen paper towels and put into an ovenproof dish. Brush over a little melted butter or olive oil and cover with foil. Leave in a cool place or the fridge. Vegetables can be prepared in this way 24 hours in advance.

When you want to serve them, season with salt and pepper and put the dish (still covered with foil) on the floor of the Roasting Oven for 15–20 minutes. Open the door and when you hear the fat spitting they should be ready. Serve immediately. You can easily do all your vegetables this way and group them together in an ovenproof serving dish.

potatoes

get-ahead roast potatoes

Prepare the potatoes in the usual way: peel, parboil on the Boiling Plate for 8 minutes, drain and fluff up by putting the lid on the pan and shaking. Put the dripping or other fat into the half- or full-size baking tray and place on the floor of the Roasting Oven to heat up. When the fat is smoking, add the potatoes, baste with the fat and cook on the floor of the Roasting Oven for 25 minutes. Take them out of the oven, turn them over, remove all but 1 tablespoon of the fat and let them cool. Cover them with foil and put aside until ready to finish off. They can be prepared up to this point 24 hours ahead of time. Do not refrigerate.

Remove the foil, and then put the potatoes back into the Roasting Oven 25 minutes before you want to serve them to finish off. Serve straight away. Timings may have to be adjusted to suit the size of the vegetables.

traditional roast potatoes

Line the large roasting tin with Bake-O-Glide and put about 2 heaped tablespoons of dripping or goose fat into it. Slide it onto the Roasting Oven floor until it is really hot and smoking. Bring the potatoes up to the boil in a saucepan of water on the Boiling Plate and cook for 5–8 minutes or until they start to give a little around the edges. Drain off all the water and, with a lid on the saucepan, shake it so that the potatoes become roughed up on the outside. Remove the tin from the oven and put it on the Simmering Plate. Add the potatoes to the hot fat. Baste them and move the tin back to the floor of the Roasting Oven for about 50 minutes or until they are crisp.

mashed potato

Jazz up everyday mash by adding different flavours – sometimes
I mix in a whole pack of garlic cream cheese or squeeze in some
roasted garlic cloves and mash them all up together.

Put the potatoes into a saucepan of water and bring to the boil on
the Boiling Plate. Boil for 3 minutes. Take the pan off the heat and
drain off all the water. Replace the lid and transfer to the
Simmering Oven for 20–30 minutes. When the potatoes are tender,
break them up with a knife or a potato ricer. Mash in butter and
crème fraîche. Season with lots of salt and black pepper. If the
potatoes are too stiff, add some more crème fraîche or a little milk.

baked potatoes

Wash the potatoes and set them on a grid shelf on the third
set of runners in the Roasting Oven for 45–60 minutes (the
cooking time very much depends on the size of the potatoes).

aga oven chips

Peel the potatoes and cut into thick strips. Soak them in cold water for 10 minutes and drain very well on a tea towel. The drier they are the better. Put the potatoes into a large bowl and pour in some sunflower oil – about 1 tablespoon for every 2 potatoes. Toss the potatoes in the oil, making sure they are evenly coated. Spread the potatoes on a large baking tray and cook them on the Roasting Oven floor for 35–45 minutes, turning occasionally, until they are brown and crisp on all sides. Remove from the oven, sprinkle generously with salt and serve. The ladies at my local W.I. love these!

new potatoes

Place the potatoes in a large pan of salted water. Bring to the boil on the Boiling Plate for 3 minutes. Drain off all the water, cover and transfer the pan to the Simmering Oven for about 30 minutes or until tender.

drying fruit and veg in the aga

This is where the 4-oven Aga really comes into its own. However, it is just as easy with a 2-oven Aga.

Slice the fruit or vegetables into 1–2 cm slices or into halves or quarters. Lay them on a shallow baking tray lined with Bake-O-Glide. Slide the tray into the Warming Oven in a 4-oven Aga for 6–8 hours or overnight. The juicier the fruit, the longer it will take to dry out. In a 2-oven Aga slide the tray onto the third set of runners in the Simmering Oven for 3–6 hours.

Leave mushrooms whole and start them in the Simmering or Warming Oven, then transfer to the lid of the Boiling Plate, protected by a tea towel or an Aga circular chef's pad until they are really dry. Store in an airtight bag or jar and rehydrate with boiling water when you want to use. Some vegetables can also be stored in olive oil, either with or without herbs.

aga dried tomatoes

Remove any stalks from tomatoes, cut in half, remove seeds
and lay them cut side up on a piece of Bake-O-Glide on a
baking tray. Drizzle over some olive oil, a little salt and
pepper and a sprinkling of caster sugar if desired. Place them
in the Simmering Oven for approximately 5–6 hours, do not
let them brown, and keep checking. When the tomatoes are
firm and dry, take them out and cool. Sterilise a jar and put
the cooled tomatoes in with some basil, garlic, thyme or any
other herb you fancy, cover them with good olive oil and seal.
Store them in the fridge where they will keep for up to three
months unopened.

as adam
said to
eve...

aga preserving

There are a few golden rules when making jams, jellies and marmalades. Make them when your Aga is at its hottest, such as first thing in the morning. Always use dry, unblemished fruit. All equipment must be scrupulously clean. Jars and lids must be sterilised. If you have a dishwasher, put them through a high heat cycle, then place on a baking tray and put in the Simmering Oven for 10–15 minutes. Keep them warm when you pour in the jam. Seal jars when hot.

Warm the sugar and fruits in the Simmering or Warming Oven before using. If a recipe calls for a fruit that needs to be cooked before adding the sugar, do it in the Simmering Oven. Use as little water as possible and cover the fruit with a tightly fitting lid. Bring to the boil on the Boiling Plate, then transfer to the Simmering Oven until it is ready.

Skim the scum off frequently when the jam is boiling or add a small knob of butter to disperse it.

To test for a good set, put a few saucers into a freezer before you start to cook the jam. After the first 20 minutes or so of rapid boiling, take a saucer out of the freezer and drop a small spoonful of the jam onto the cold saucer. Allow it to cool for a minute, and then push your finger through the jam. If it wrinkles, it is ready; if not, boil the jam for a few minutes more. Carry on testing until a set has been reached. Always remove the jam from the heat when you are testing so that if it is ready you will not overcook the jam.

poaching fruit

Place the prepared fruit in a saucepan. Add any flavourings such as honey, sugar, spices or a cinnamon stick, and just enough water to cover the fruit. Cover the pan with a lid, place on the Boiling Plate and bring to the boil. Transfer to the Simmering Oven for 2–3 hours or until the fruit is soft and plump.

baked apples

Core the apples and score the peel horizontally around the middle of the fruit. Place in a roasting tin lined with Bake-O-Glide. Stuff the apples with sultanas, marzipan or any filling of your choice and top with generous knobs of butter. Slide the tin onto the third set of runners in the Roasting Oven and bake for 30–35 minutes or until the apples are tender but still hold their shape. If they brown too much, move to the fourth set of runners and place the Cold Plain Shelf on the second set of runners. For 4-oven Aga owners, bake in the Baking Oven for 40–45 minutes.

a piece of cake

baking in the aga is as easy as pie

Baking is where the Cold Plain Shelf comes into its own. So many Aga owners use it as an extra shelf, rendering it completely useless for the job it is intended for. I really do recommend buying a second Cold Plain Shelf if you are a keen baker. It must be kept outside the Aga, not inside one of the ovens. The Cold Plain Shelf will give you a moderate oven for about 20–40 minutes. So if you are a 2-oven Aga owner, for cakes requiring more than 40 minutes use a Cake Baker. For 4-oven Aga owners, use the Baking Oven, although you will notice some recipes will start in the Roasting Oven. Plan your baking when the ovens are cooler, such as after you have had a big cooking session.

As a general rule, I have found that the best positions for baking cakes are either with the grid shelf on the lowest set of runners in the Roasting Oven with the Cold Plain Shelf above on the second set of runners, or with the grid shelf on the floor of the Roasting

Oven and the Cold Plain Shelf on either the third or fourth set of
runners, depending how high the cake tin is. Most cakes (apart
from fruit cakes) take roughly 20 minutes to cook. Check the cake
regularly while it is baking; opening the oven door will not impair
the finished cake – in fact I have cooked a victoria sponge with the
oven door completely off and it was fine.

Remember: the two best positions for baking cakes are either
with the grid shelf on the lowest runners in the roasting oven
with the cold plain shelf on the second set of runners, or with
the grid shelf on the roasting oven floor with the cold plain
shelf on the third or fourth runners.

planning your baking

As it is better if the oven is a little cooler when you bake, try to plan your baking for the afternoon or after a major cooking session. Over the years I have picked up many useful tips from other Aga owners when it comes to baking. One tip is to boil the kettle and leave it on the Simmering Plate so that, with the lid up, the cooker will not be so hot. I prefer to plan my baking to follow a cooking session and I have lots of Cold Plain Shelves to keep me going.

It goes without saying that if you can make any of your dishes ahead of time, do so. Bread doughs can be made and proved for the first time then put in the fridge until you are ready to use. Prepare as much as possible in advance so that all you are doing is opening up an oven door and sliding something in. I always keep a few tart tins lined with sweet and savoury pastry in the freezer so that if I need a quick pudding or savoury tart when someone arrives unexpectedly, all I have to do is make up a filling and pop it into the oven. This is where we are lucky – blind baking simply does not feature in the Aga owner's world!

bakeware for your aga

Good-quality tins are crucial when baking, and the heavier they are, the better the results will be (see pages 63 and 65). I recommend all tins should be hard anodised items. You may find that darker coloured tins require a shorter cooking time than lighter ones (such as aluminium) because dark colours absorb heat more quickly. Loose-bottomed or spring form tins are so much easier to use.

Thin tins are unsuitable for Aga use because the heat passes through them too quickly, so the outside of the cake may burn before the centre is cooked.

a word about tarts...

Pastry-lined tart tins do not need to be blind-baked. Line the tin with raw pastry, add filling and set on the Roasting Oven floor with the cold plain shelf above.

the oven reach (see page 63) is essential for pulling out tarts, breads and pizzas from the roasting oven floor

a word about fruit cakes...

When it comes to baking your fruit cake, the best oven in the world is the 2-oven Aga Simmering Oven. Prepare your fruit cake recipe as usual and then place the tin on the third set of runners in the Simmering Oven. On average, a 20 cm round fruit cake will take anything from 4 to 10 hours. The reasons for the timing variation are that no two Aga cookers are the same and the newer ones have better insulation. My standard fruit cake recipe in the Simmering Oven takes about 6 hours.

Owners of a 4-oven Aga may find their Simmering Oven is slower than a 2-oven Aga Simmering Oven. The cake will probably cook better if started in the Baking Oven for 45–60 minutes, then transferred to the Simmering Oven in as high a position as possible and cooked for anywhere from 4–10 hours or even longer in some cases. Another trick is to use the large grill rack from the large roasting tin. Put the grill rack directly onto the Simmering Oven floor and put the cake tin on it for cooking. If you feel you don't need the extra boost of the Baking Oven, bake the cake in the Simmering Oven only as above.

Lining the tin with Bake-O-Glide is all the tin preparation you need. There's no need for brown paper or newspaper for lining and covering the cake. Another good method for cooking fruit cake is the Aga Cake Baker (see page 117). The only drawback is that you are restricted to the size and shape of the tins.

the cake baker

Using the Aga Cake Baker means there is no need to turn cakes during baking and no worry of them over-browning.

To use the cake baker, select the correct-sized tin and remove the trivet and cake tins from inside the cake baker. Put the outer container and lid onto the Roasting Oven floor to heat up. Pour the cake mix into the tin and remove the cake baker from the oven. Set the trivet and cake tin inside the cake baker. Replace the lid and put it on the Roasting Oven floor. Set the timer.

bc – before the cake baker

A really good baking tip for 2-oven Aga owners is to use the Cold Plain Shelf as a hot shelf. If you have a recipe that requires a longer cooking time, over 40 minutes or so, and don't have a Cake Baker you will want to move the cake from the Roasting Oven to the Simmering Oven. The best way to continue the baking is to slide the Cold Plain Shelf (even if you don't need it) into the Roasting Oven to heat up so when you need to move your cake to the Simmering Oven, you move the shelf as well. Slide the now 'hot' Plain Shelf onto the desired runner, and continue baking the cake on it. The hot plain shelf gives an extra boost of heat to the cake and oven.

a word about bread...

I rarely use a loaf tin for bread. I make my bread into rustic shapes and bake directly on the Roasting oven floor. Take a shallow baking tray and turn it over. Put a sheet of Bake-O-Glide on top of the upturned baking tray and transfer the shaped dough on top. Place the baking tray halfway into the oven, then carefully slide the tray out, leaving the Bake-O-Glide and bread in the oven.

for the best bread crust

Baking bread is fantastic because the Roasting Oven in an Aga is just like a baker's oven. Buy a small cup-sized stainless steel beaker or mould. Fill it with cold water and place in the Roasting Oven when baking bread. It will create the steam which is essential in achieving a good crust. You can also splash water directly onto the Roasting Oven floor for an instant blast of steam. It's good to do this halfway through baking and just before the final 8 minutes of baking.

For a really crispy base crust, sprinkle the Bake-O-Glide with the polenta or finely sieved stale breadcrumbs and place your shaped dough on top.

pizza the action

Line a large inverted baking tray with Bake-O-Glide. Put on the shaped pizza dough and leave the tin next to the Aga for its second rising. Place the tin on the edge of the floor of the Roasting Oven and pull the Bake-O-Glide towards the back of the oven and the tray away, so you are left with dough on the Bake-O-Glide on the oven floor. Use my Oven Reach like a pizza peel to remove the pizza from the oven.

baking hints

- Plan to do your baking when you know your Aga will be slightly cooler, such as after a large cooking session.
- Use heavy-based tins for all your baking and cake-making.
- Use Bake-O-Glide to line cake tins.
- Use the Roasting Oven floor to bake bread.
- Use the Simmering Plate covered with a round piece of Bake-O-Glide to cook pancakes, drop scones and tuiles.

- Warm flour and sugar needed for recipes either at the back of the Aga or in the Simmering and Warming Ovens.
- Buy two Cold Plain Shelves – you can cool them down quickly by running them under cold water, but having an extra one will save this task.
- Use the black surface area of the top of the Aga to melt butter or chocolate for baking.
- Prove yeast-based recipes and bread dough next to the Aga – it can cut the proving time in half in some cases.
- Keep a kettle of boiling water going on the top of the Simmering Plate to lower an oven temperature.
- Refresh stale bread by spraying with water and baking it in the Roasting Oven for 5 minutes.

general baking positions and timings

Bread: Roasting Oven floor.

Cheesecake: grid shelf on the Roasting Oven floor with the Cold Plain Shelf above for 5–10 minutes, then move the now hot plain shelf to the Simmering Oven and put the cheesecake on top of it for 35–45 minutes. You can start it in the Baking Oven for 15–20 minutes, and then move to the Simmering Oven.

Cookies and biscuits: fourth set of runners in the Roasting Oven or third set of runners in the Baking Oven.

Frozen bread: fourth set of runners in the Roasting Oven; grid shelf on the floor of the Roasting Oven.

Frozen pastry cases: Roasting Oven floor.

Melting chocolate/butter: back of Aga on black enamel top, on the Warming Plate or in the Simmering Oven for 10 minutes.

Muffins: grid shelf on the floor of the Roasting Oven or fourth set of runners with the Cold Plain Shelf on the runners above; Baking Oven on third set of runners.

Pancakes: directly on the Simmering Plate surface using a piece of Bake-O-Glide or wipe a small amount of oil onto the surface.

Pizza: floor of the Roasting Oven for approximately 12 minutes.

Popovers: heat tin on the Roasting Oven floor, pour in batter, then move up to third set of runners.

Scones: third set of runners in the Roasting Oven.

Sponge cakes: grid shelf on the Roasting Oven floor with the Cold Plain Shelf on the third set of runners.

common baking problems solved

Cracked top
The cake has usually been baked in too hot an oven or it has been positioned too close to the top of the oven or the Plain Shelf. The top of the cake sets and therefore makes it very difficult for the gas to spread evenly around the cake.

Cake with a raised middle
This happens when a cake is put in too hot an oven, then moved to too low a temperature before the outside of the cake has a chance to set, or the mixture hasn't been creamed enough.

Burnt bottom
The most obvious reason for a burnt cake bottom is too thin a tin. The other problem that can occur is that not enough air circulates around the cake tin as can be the case if you use the Plain Shelf instead of a grid rack. For fruit cakes and cakes requiring long

baking times, first start the cake off on the grid shelf then, when the cake is set, transfer it to a hot Plain Shelf. To cool an oven and for extra absorption of heat in an oven, place a roasting tin containing either clean sand or water on the floor or on the lower shelf.

Sunken centre

There are three reasons for this happening: too much raising agent, too hot an oven and a third reason which happily doesn't apply to Aga owners – slamming a conventional oven door soon after the cake has gone in lets in a sudden rush of cold air and changes the pressure in the oven, shaking the air out before the cake has a chance to set.

cooking for crowds

When cooking for a crowd or for a special occasion, remember that a lot of food can be cooked in advance and reheated when ready to serve. For example, roast potatoes can be roasted for 20 minutes, then taken out, left overnight in a cool area, then blasted in the Roasting Oven for 20 minutes (see page 96). Yorkshire pudding can be done in the morning when the Roasting Oven is at its hottest, then reheated for 8 minutes before serving.

the full aga breakfast

A proper breakfast can be one of the hardest meals to get absolutely right – everything must be cooked to order, usually for large numbers of people. Co-ordinating toast, eggs, bacon and so on can become a nightmare, but not for the Aga owner!

1 Depending on how many you are cooking for, use either the half-size roasting tin or the full-size one. Line it with Bake-O-Glide, and put the mushrooms and tomato halves, cut side up, on the bottom of the tin. Drizzle over a little oil and season. Place the grill rack on top and put the sausages on the rack over the mushrooms and tomatoes (do not prick the sausages).

2 Slide the tin onto the first set of runners in the Roasting Oven, and cook for 10 minutes. Then take the tin out of the oven, turn the sausages and lay the bacon rashers on the grill rack. Put it back into the Roasting Oven for a further 10 minutes. Depending on the thickness of the bacon and the size of the sausages, you may need to adjust the timings.

3 When everything is cooked, take the tin out of the oven and put the bacon, sausages, tomatoes and mushrooms onto a warmed platter, cover with foil and transfer to the Simmering Oven to keep warm while you cook the eggs (see right). If you want well-done bacon, after you remove the sausages, tomatoes and mushrooms to the platter, take off the grill rack and put the bacon on the bottom of the tin. Place the tin on the floor of the Roasting Oven and let the bacon cook to your liking.

4 To make fried bread, do it in exactly the same way as for well-done bacon, adding a little more oil to the tin if necessary. It will take about 5 minutes for each side.

eggs

fried eggs

There are two ways of cooking fried eggs – either in the Aga or on the Aga.

In the Aga: When you remove the sausages, bacon and so on from the tin, add a little more oil to the tin and put it on the Roasting Oven floor to get really hot. When the oil is hot, crack the eggs into the tin one at a time. The large tin will take about 6 large eggs and the half-size tin about 3 large eggs. Baste the eggs with the fat and put the tin back into the oven for 3 minutes or until they are done to your liking.

On the Aga: Open the Simmering Plate lid and either grease it with a little oil, or use a round pre-cut circle of Bake-O-Glide and put it directly onto the Simmering Plate surface. Drizzle a little oil onto a piece of kitchen paper and rub it over the plate. Crack the egg onto the hot surface and close the lid. The egg will cook in about

2 minutes. The Simmering Plate surface can take about 3 large eggs at a time. (If you have an Aga with a dented lid, check to see whether it touches the top of the egg when you close it. If it does, leave the lid open. The egg will take a little longer to cook.)

poached eggs
Fill a saucepan with water and place on the Simmering Plate. When it has reached a gentle simmer, swirl the water with a spoon to form a whirlpool. Crack the egg into the water and poach for about 2 minutes. Eggs must be really fresh.

scrambled eggs
Cook scrambled eggs in melted butter in a non-stick saucepan on the Simmering Plate.

See page 146 for Aga toast.

sunday lunch

When cooking a traditional Sunday lunch with all the trimmings, it's essential to plan ahead – see my tips on page 33. Try cooking the Aga get-ahead vegetables (see page 95).

yorkshire pudding

Prepare and cook the Yorkshire pudding earlier in the morning and set aside, then simply re-heat for 8 minutes in the Roasting Oven.

christmas lunch

Aga owners are always worried about running out of heat so to prevent this, write out a preparation schedule and a cooking timetable. This timetable is based on a 7 kg turkey, to be served at 2pm. Note that I cook my stuffing in a dish, not inside the bird. This way it can be made in advance and reheated.

7:30am
Remove the turkey from the refrigerator and pop a halved onion inside and season the cavity.

8:15am
Put the turkey in the oven and baste with melted butter every 30 minutes. If you are using the Warming Oven in a 4-oven Aga, put in the required plates and serving dishes.

11:30am
Prepare bacon rolls and chipolatas. Re-heat bread sauce (made the day before) and place it in a jug with butter on top to melt over the surface, keep warm.

12:00
Start steaming the Christmas pudding. Bring to the boil on the Boiling Plate, then transfer to the Simmering Oven for 3 hours.

12:45pm
If you are cooking your vegetables conventionally, do roast potatoes and prepare saucepans of boiling water for any other vegetables. Re-heat stuffing.

1:15pm
Remove turkey from oven, cover loosely with foil and let it rest. Make gravy (see page 140) and keep warm.

1:30pm
Check chipolatas and bacon rolls, remove and keep warm. Put in 'get ahead' roast potatoes (see page 96).

1:45pm
Put sprouts on to cook or put in 'get ahead' blanched vegetables (see page 95). While they are cooking, transfer the other food into serving dishes and carve the turkey. Check Christmas pudding.

2:00pm
Serve Christmas lunch.

aga basics

These are the hints and tips and basic recipes every Aga cook wants to have in their repertoire.

stock

This is the basic Aga method for making stock. See overleaf for chicken, game and fish stock.

Roast off the meat bones in the Roasting Oven for about 45 minutes or until brown, then put them into a large pot and cover with cold water. Add herbs, seasoning, half an onion, a chopped up carrot, celery, garlic and anything else you fancy (but not starch-based vegetables such as potatoes). Bring to the boil on the Boiling Plate and boil rapidly for 5–10 minutes. Cover with a lid and transfer to the Simmering Oven for at least 6 hours or overnight. Skim off the fat and strain through a sieve. Store in the fridge for up to a week, bringing it to the boil before using, or freeze for up to 3 months.

For chicken and game stock:
Use a whole carcass, but do not brown. Start it in cold water.

For fish stock:
Do not brown the fish bones, and only cook for about an hour.
Keep for 3 days in the fridge.

gravy

It doesn't matter what sort of meat you are roasting as the method
is still the same. I use onions as a rack for the meat to sit on while
it is roasting.

You can vary the fruit jelly to suit the meat the gravy is to
accompany, such as apple jelly for pork or mint jelly for lamb.
You can use less stock for thicker gravy, or more for a thinner
consistency. The quality of the stock is paramount – if you use
inferior stock you will end up with inferior gravy. Always use
home-made stock (see page 139).

Cut two onions in half and rest the joint on top. When the joint is cooked, remove it from the tin, cover with foil and let it rest for 15–20 minutes. Spoon off any excess fat from the tin, leaving about 1–2 tablespoons with the meat juices and onions.

While the meat is resting, put the tin directly onto the Simmering Plate and bring the juices to a simmer. Add 1 tablespoon of flour to the fat, onions and meat juices and whisk it in. Keep whisking until the flour absorbs all of the fat, adding a little more flour if necessary. Whisking constantly so that there are no lumps, pour in about 100 ml of wine (optional). Add a tablespoon of redcurrant jelly. Still whisking, pour in about 500 ml of stock.

Bring the gravy to a rapid simmer and cook for about 5 minutes. Add salt and pepper to taste. It is very important to cook out the flour (and wine, if using). Strain the gravy into a warmed serving jug and keep hot at the back of the Aga or in the Simmering or Warming Oven.

rice

This is such an easy way to cook rice and once you try it you won't cook rice any other way! It is entirely up to you whether you rinse the rice. As a general rule, use just under double the amount of liquid to rice. To make knockout rice, fry an onion in a little oil and butter until soft then add the rice, stirring well to coat every grain with the oil/butter. Pour in home-made stock and season with salt and pepper. Cook as below. When the rice is ready, stir in a generous knob of butter.

Put the rice, water and salt into a large saucepan and bring it up to the boil on the Boiling Plate. Stir it once, then cover with a lid and put it on the floor of the Simmering Oven for 18–20 minutes (brown rice will take 30–40 minutes). Remove it from the oven and take the lid off. Fluff up the rice with a fork and cover the pan with a clean tea towel to absorb some of the steam, and then serve.

polenta

This speedy method of cooking quick-cook polenta will serve 4.

Bring 500 ml water to the boil in a pan on the Boiling Plate and add a teaspoon of salt and 3 tablespoons of olive oil. Pour in 120 g quick-cook polenta and stir well. Transfer to the Simmering Plate and cook for about 1 minute, then put a lid on the pan and place on the floor of the Simmering Oven for 15–20 minutes or until the mixture is very thick and dense. Beat in 120 g grated Parmesan. Spread out onto a flat surface, such as a plate lined with Bake-O-Glide, and cool completely. This can be done up to a day in advance if you wish.

To grill the polenta, cut it into wedges and heat a grill pan on the floor of the Roasting Oven. When the pan is really hot, brush a little olive oil over the polenta wedges, take pan out of the oven, place on the Boiling Plate and grill each side for 2–3 minutes until they are crispy and brown.

pasta

Pasta can be cooked very easily on the Boiling or Simmering Plate. Bring a large pot of water to the boil, generously add salt, then when the water reaches a rolling boil, add the pasta and cook for however many minutes the packet instructions say.

---

roasting coffee beans

To roast green coffee beans, spread the beans out in the large roasting tin. Hang the tin on the first set of runners in the Roasting Oven for 25–30 minutes or until the oils start to run and the beans turn golden brown. Shake the pan three or four times during cooking to roast evenly.

---

porridge

For each serving, place 75 g pinhead oatmeal and 600 ml water in a pan and bring to the boil on the Boiling Plate, then transfer to the Simmering Plate for 2 minutes. Meanwhile, put the grid shelf on the Simmering Oven floor. Cover the pan with a lid and place on the grid shelf. Leave overnight. Stir well before serving and add brown sugar and cream.

As overnight can mean anything from 6 to 12 hours, another way to cook the porridge is to follow these instructions but put it at the back of the Aga on the hot black enamel surface instead of inside the Simmering Oven.

Keep salt in a salt box next to the Aga and it will remain dry.

toast

To make toast, put a slice of bread in the Aga toasting rack and
place it on the Boiling Plate. Close the lid but keep an eye on it as
it will toast very quickly; turn over to do the other side.

To stop very fresh bread from sticking to the toaster, heat the rack
first on the Boiling Plate before inserting the bread. If you like
crispy toast, leave the Boiling Plate lid open.

breadcrumbs

To dry breadcrumbs, sprinkle them on a baking tray and 'cook' in
the Simmering Oven for 10 minutes then, protecting the lid with a
tea towel, place the tray on top and leave there until the
breadcrumbs are completely dry.Four-oven owners can use the
Warming Oven.

croûtons

Cut bread into 2-cm cubes. Toss them in olive oil, making sure they are well coated. Spread them on a baking tray and bake on the first set of runners in the Roasting Oven for 8–10 minutes. Keep an eye on them as they burn very easily. Cool on a plate lined with kitchen towel.

toasted sandwiches

These are so easy and are great for ravenous teenagers! Butter two slices of bread. Place your filling (such as ham and grated cheese) on one unbuttered side and top with the other slice, again buttered side facing outwards, and press together. Place a piece of Bake-O-Glide on the Simmering Plate and lift the sandwich onto it. Close the lid and cook for 2–3 minutes. Open the lid, flip the sandwich over, close the lid and cooker for a further 2–3 minutes or until the bread is golden.

infused oils

These are useful for jazzing up plain dishes and for salad dressings, and are so easy to make in the Aga. Oils will last for up to 3 months in the refrigerator. Bring to room temperature at the back of the Aga when you are ready to use.

lemon oil
Use for garnishing salads, in salad dressings and fish dishes.

Cut the peel away from an organic lemon. Bruise 4 stalks of lemongrass by bashing with a rolling pin. Put the peel and lemongrass into a saucepan. Pour over 1 litre grapeseed oil and 100 ml good-quality olive oil. Bring to the boil on the Boiling Plate, then transfer to the Simmering Oven for 30 minutes. Remove from the oven, cover with cling film and stand at room temperature overnight. Strain into a container, adding one of the stalks of lemongrass, and store.

chilli oil

Use this drizzled over pizzas, in salad dressings or when cooking spicy dishes.

Crush 10 dried chillies and put them into a saucepan. Pour over 500 ml grapeseed oil and 500 ml olive oil and bring to a simmer on the Simmering Plate. Take the saucepan off the heat and leave the oil to infuse for 5–7 days. Strain into a bottle and store.

melting chocolate and butter

Use all of the black surface area on the top of the Aga – it is great for melting butter or chocolate. Break up the chocolate into pieces; put it into a bowl and stand it to the left of the Boiling Plate and it will melt in no time at all. Warm flour and sugar for baking here as well.

at your convenience...

The everyday reality for many of us is that during the week dinner is just as likely to come out of a packet as it is from the latest cookbook. This is where the Aga comes in – just pop the foil packet on a baking tray and slide it onto the third or fourth set of runners in the Roasting Oven and dinner is ready in no time at all.

because the aga is always hot and always ready, the aga waits for you – you never have to wait for the aga

Poppadums can be cooked directly on the Boiling Plate with the lid down; they are ready in seconds.

frozen foods at a glance

Frozen breads: third set of runners in the Roasting Oven for 10–15 minutes, covered with foil if browning too much.
Frozen fish fingers/chicken nuggets/chips: start on the Roasting Oven floor, then move to third set of runners (total cooking time about 10–12 minutes).
Frozen pizza: directly on the Roasting Oven floor.

wine
To bring cold red wine up to temperature, stand the bottle on a folded tea towel at the back of the Aga on the black enamel or wrap it in a tea towel and lay it on the Simmering Plate lid.

hidden talents

The Aga is not just a wonderful cooker – it also has hidden talents and can sometimes act like an extra pair of hands in the kitchen. One of the best things about this cooker is its ability to do the ironing!

aga 'ironing'

To 'iron' items such as sheets, pillowcases, hankies, tea towels, vests and so on, fold the newly washed and spun laundry. Smooth and press in creases firmly by hand and place them on the Simmering Plate lid. Turn them over when one side is dry.

Press sheets by hanging them over the chrome rail (but take care not to obstruct the air vents on the burner door), then fold and press firmly when almost dry and transfer to the lid of the Simmering Plate to press.

Never place laundry on the Boiling Plate lid as it may become scorched. Take care not to drape washing over the handles of the lids.

and another thing . . .

- Stand awkward gadgets such as cheese graters and garlic crushers at the back of the Aga and they will dry in all those hard-to-reach corners.

- Dry glassware and decanters on a tea towel at the back of the Aga.

- Store your wooden spoons in a container near the Aga as it will keep them dry.

- Heat unusual-shaped dishes at the back of the Aga. To warm large platters, place a tea towel underneath them to prevent them slipping and stand them upright, propped against the back or the side of the Aga.

- Opening stubborn new jar lids could not be simpler. Invert the jar top onto the Simmering Plate for a few seconds and you will hear it release. Protect your hands with a tea towel before touching the hot metal lid.

- Stuff wet shoes or boots with newspaper and leave to dry near the Aga, or if you have a 4-oven Aga, place them in the Warming Oven.

- Newly glued items, such as models and glued china, dry quicker when placed on a protected Simmering Plate lid.

- Seal milky flower stems on the Boiling Plate.

- Birdseed or pet food can often become damp if left out. Simply place it on the back of the Aga and it will be dry in no time.

aga animals

Rather endearingly, all animals just seem to love sitting right in front of an Aga.

We have all heard about farmers' wives who have revived every animal known to man – chicks, orphaned lambs and calves, rabbits, guinea pigs, kittens, you name it and it has been resuscitated and warmed either in, on or in front of the Aga. I have even heard about a reptile who likes to coil up on a covered lid!

muffin's munchies

This is my recipe for home-made dog biscuits. (Muffin is my dog, she's a Jack Russell.)

120 g ox liver
1 large egg
120 g wholemeal flour

Whizz up all the ingredients in a food processor until smoothish. Line a tin with Bake-O-Glide or greaseproof paper and spread the mix in the tin. Bake in the Roasting Oven on the fourth set of runners with the Cold Plain Shelf above for about 10–15 minutes or until hard. Do not burn. Remove from the tin immediately and cool. Cut into chunks or biscuits and keep covered in the fridge for up to a week, or freeze. Label well!

the jasons and the aga-naut

The Aga can be found in all sorts of unexpected places, from the South Pole to South Africa, but few are as unusual as the Aga that occasionally appears in the *Viz* comic strip 'The Jasons and the Aga-Naut'. The story follows the Jason family and their extraordinary cooker. In one issue the Jason family and their Aga visited Wales. Here is a snippet from the tale:

'Roaring down the River Conwy in North Wales was the most incredible paddle-steamer you had ever seen. Belonging to the Jason family from Gloucestershire, it was a gigantic Aga cooker which had been built by the father, Rupert Jason. And now Rupert was taking his wife Jocasta and their two children, Laura and Ashley, on a thrilling holiday – an expedition deep into the uncharted heart of darkest Wales.'

aga rules!

- Cook as much as possible in the ovens – the Aga is designed for 80 per cent of cooking to be done in the ovens and 20 per cent on top.
- Think before you lift your lids.
- Use Amy Willcock's Rangeware by Mermaid specially designed for range cooking.
- Keep a damp cloth at the ready to wipe up spills as and when they happen.
- Make family and friends Aga-aware – don't drag pans over the enamel surface or over the chrome lids.
- Don't touch that dial once the correct setting has been achieved – leave it alone!
- Service regularly with a recognised Aga dealer.
- Keep the Plain Shelf cold, buy an extra one for batch baking and use Rangeware cake tins.
- Buy extra Rangeware roasting tins in full and half sizes and use them as much as possible.
- Don't let animals (or bottoms warming on the rail) stop you from getting to the Aga!

useful contacts

Amy Willcock's own range of cookware called Rangeware is produced by Mermaid. For your nearest stockist, please telephone 0121 554 2001 or email sales@mermaidcookware.com.

Amy Willcock's own website is www.amywillcock.co.uk.

The Aga website is www.agalinks.co.uk. The Aga-Rayburn telephone number for general information is 01952 642000.

For information on Aga cookers in the USA, contact Bonnie Fleming on (001) 704 333 9234, or write to her at 651 Museum Drive, Charlotte, North Carolina 28207, USA.

further reading

Also available from the same author and published by Ebury Press (www.randomhouse.co.uk):

Aga Cooking

Amy Willcock's Aga Baking

index